COMFORT

COMFORT

Warren W. Wiersbe

VICTOR BOOKS

A DIVISION OF SCRIPTURE PRESS PUBLICATIONS INC.
USA CANADA ENGLAND

Unless otherwise noted, Scripture quotations are from the *Holy Bible: New International Version®*. Copyright © 1973, 1978, 1984 by International Bible Society. Used by permission of Zondervan Publishing House. All rights reserved. Quotations marked KJV are from the *Authorized (King James) Version*.

Editor: Afton Rorvik
Designer: Grace K. Chan Mallette

Library of Congress Cataloging-in-Publication Data

Wiersbe, Warren W.
   Comfort: a 30-day devotional / by Warren W. Wiersbe.
     p.   cm.
   Each devotional is adapted from a chapter in Be comforted, a Bible study on Isaiah.
   ISBN 1-56476-402-8
   1. Bible. O.T. Isaiah—Meditations 2. Devotional calendars.
   I. Wiersbe, Warren W. Comfort. II. Title.
   BS1515.4.W54 1995
   224'.106—dc20   95-7686
                                                                                       CIP

© 1995 by Victor Books/SP Publications, Inc. All rights reserved. Printed in the United States of America.

1 2 3 4 5 6 7 8 9 10 Printing / Year 99 98 97 96 95

No part of this book may be reproduced without written permission, except for brief quotations in books and critical reviews. For information write Victor Books, 1825 College Avenue, Wheaton, Illinois 60187.

If you are studying *Be Comforted* in a Sunday School class or small group, this 30-Day Devotional will complement your study. Each devotional is adapted from a chapter in *Be Comforted*. The following chart indicates the correlation. You may, of course, use this book without reference to *Be Comforted*.

Be Comforted Book Chapter	Comfort 30-Day Devotional
Preface	**Day 1**
1	**Days 2 and 3**
2	**Days 4 and 5**
3	**Days 6 and 7**
4	**Days 8 and 9**
5	**Days 10 and 11**
6	**Days 12, 13, and 14**
7	**Days 15 and 16**
Interlude	**Day 17**
8	**Days 18 and 19**
Interlude	**Day 20**
9	**Days 21 and 22**
10	**Days 23 and 24**
11	**Days 25 and 26**
12	**Days 27 and 28**
13	**Days 29 and 30**

INTRODUCTION

It's too bad that our English word *comfort* has lost its original meaning of "with strength." The purpose of comfort isn't to pamper and protect us but to strengthen us and enable us to carry the burdens of life and serve the Lord effectively.

God isn't a doting grandparent who shelters us from problems and "kisses" our bruises to "make them well." He's a loving Father who wants us to mature and become more like Jesus Christ; and for that, we must face new challenges and depend on new strength from above.

"O, do not pray for easy lives," said Phillips Brooks. "Pray to be stronger men! Do not pray for tasks equal to your powers. Pray for powers equal to your tasks!" (The Rt. Rev. William Scarlett, D.D., *Phillips Brooks: Selected Sermons* E.P. Dutton & Company, Inc., p. 352). That's what God's comfort is all about: power from God to meet the demands of life *and to grow because of them.* If we don't grow, we can't tackle bigger tasks and serve God in harder places.

The Prophet Isaiah lived in a day similar to our own. The nations were frequently at war; political schemes and alliances changed from day to day; the economy was frequently threatened; the people practiced a routine religion that covered up their hidden idolatry; and few people really wanted to hear the Word of the Lord.

Into this discouraging scene came Isaiah, sharing the comfort – the strength – of the Lord. His major theme was salvation. His major purpose was to give strength to a people who were prone to drift with the current and depend on everything but the Lord.

As you walk with Isaiah, learn to receive God's comfort, *and learn to share it with others.* They need it too.

—Warren W. Wiersbe

*My thanks to Stan Campbell,
who compiled the contents of this book
and added thought-provoking questions
to enrich your personal growth.*

DAY 1

Read **Isaiah 40:1**

Much Upheaval; Much Comfort

"Isaiah is great for two reasons," wrote William Sanford LaSor in his fascinating book *Great Personalities of the Old Testament* (Revell, p. 136): "He lived in momentous days, in critical days of international upheaval, and he wrote what many consider to be the greatest book in the Old Testament."

"We see Isaiah move with fearless dignity through the chaos of his day," wrote E.M. Blaiklock, "firm in his quiet faith, sure in his God" (*Handbook of Bible People*, Scripture Union, p. 329).

Isaiah is the prophet we need to hear today as he cries out God's message above the din of world upheaval, "Comfort, comfort My people." The English word *comfort* comes from two Latin words that together mean "with strength." When Isaiah says to us, "Be comforted!" it is not a word of pity but of power. God's comfort does not weaken us; it strengthens us. God is not indulging us but empowering us. "In quietness and confidence shall be your strength."

As we study Isaiah's book, we shall meet not only

> *"Comfort, comfort My people,*
> *says your God"*
> *(Isaiah 40:1).*

....

this outstanding prophet, but also some mighty kings and rulers, and we shall witness the rise and fall of magnificent kingdoms. We shall see God's people chastened and then restored. But above all else, we shall see the Lord Jesus Christ, God's "Suffering Servant," as He does the will of God and suffers and dies for the sins of the world.

Applying God's Truth:

1. Can you think back to a time when God's comfort gave you much strength? What did you learn from that experience?

2. What situation are you currently facing in which you are in great need of God's comfort?

3. What are your goals (or hopes) as you read through the Book of Isaiah?

DAY 2

Read **Isaiah 1:1**

A Prophecy You Can Count On

The name "Isaiah" means "salvation of the Lord," and salvation (deliverance) is the key theme of his book. He wrote concerning *five different acts of deliverance* that God would perform: (1) the deliverance of Judah from Assyrian invasion (chaps. 36—37); (2) the deliverance of the nation from Babylonian captivity (chap. 40); (3) the future deliverance of the Jews from worldwide dispersion among the Gentiles (chaps. 11—12); (4) the deliverance of lost sinners from judgment (chap. 53); and (5) the final deliverance of creation from the bondage of sin when the kingdom is established (chaps. 60; 66:17ff).

Sir Winston Churchill was once asked to give the qualifications a person needed in order to succeed in politics, and he replied: "It is the ability to foretell what is going to happen tomorrow, next week, next month, and next year. And to have the ability afterwards to explain why it didn't happen."

Because God's prophets were correct *all of the time*, they didn't have to explain away their mistakes. "If what a prophet proclaims in the name of the Lord does not take place or come true," wrote Moses, "that

"The vision concerning Judah and Jerusalem that Isaiah son of Amoz saw" (Isaiah 1:1).

....

is a message the Lord has not spoken" (Deut. 18:22). Isaiah wrote: "To the law and to the testimony! If they do not speak according to this word, they have no light of dawn" (8:20). Isaiah was a man who had God's light, and he was not afraid to let it shine.

Applying God's Truth:

1. Isaiah's name means "salvation of the Lord." If you were given a name to reflect your spiritual goals or mission, what do you think it might be?

2. In what ways do you think others see God's light shine from your life?

3. What are five "acts of deliverance" that you wish God would perform in your life?

DAY 3

Read *Isaiah 1:2-4*

Isaiah: A Personality Profile

What kind of man was Isaiah the prophet? As you read his prophecy, you will discover that he was *a man in touch with God*. He saw God's Son and God's glory, he heard God's message, and he sought to bring the nation back to God before it was too late.

Isaiah was a man who *loved his nation*. He was a patriot with a true love for his country, pleading with Judah to return to God and warning kings when their foreign policy was contrary to God's will.

He was also a man who *hated sin and sham religion*. His favorite name for God is "the Holy One of Israel," and he uses it twenty-five times in his book. (It is used only five times in the rest of the Old Testament.) He looked at the crowded courts of the temple and cried out, "They have forsaken the LORD; they have spurned the Holy One of Israel and turned their backs on Him" (v. 4). Jehovah was holy, but the nation was sinful, and Isaiah called the people to repent.

Isaiah was certainly a *courageous man*. Unafraid to denounce kings and priests, and unwavering when

> *"The ox knows his master,*
> *the donkey his owner's manger,*
> *but Israel does not know,*
> *My people do not understand"*
> *(Isaiah 1:3).*

public opinion went against him, he boldly declared the Word of God.

He was a man *skilled in communicating God's truth.* Not content with merely declaring facts, Isaiah clothed those facts in striking language that would catch the attention of a people blind and deaf to spiritual truth. Like our Lord Jesus Christ, Isaiah knew how to stir the imagination of his listeners so that he might arouse their interest and teach them God's truth (Matt. 13:10-17).

Applying God's Truth:

1. Of all Isaiah's qualities described here, which would you say is most important for a prophet of God? Why?

2. Which of these qualities best describes *you?*

3. How do you think a person with these characteristics would fit into a nation that has "turned its back" on God?

DAY 4

Read *Isaiah 1:5–3:26*

Religion Gone Wrong

The disgusting thing about the people in Isaiah's rebellious nation is that they were a *religious people* (1:10-15). They attended temple services and brought a multitude of sacrifices to the Lord, but their hearts were far from God, and their worship was hypocritical. Judah's worship of Jehovah was iniquity, not piety. God was sick of it!

But before passing judgment on worshipers in a bygone era, perhaps we should confess the sins of the "worshiping church" today. According to researcher George Barna, 93 percent of the households in the United States contain a Bible and more than 60 percent of the people surveyed claim to be religious, but we would never know this from the way people act. One Protestant church exists for every 550 adults in America, but does all this "religion" make much difference in our sinful society?

The average church allocates about 5 percent of its budget for reaching others with the Gospel, but 30 percent for buildings and maintenance. Where churches have life and growth, such construction may be needed, but too often the building becomes "a

> *"Your hands are full of blood;*
> *wash and make yourselves clean.*
> *Take your evil deeds out of My sight!*
> *Stop doing wrong, learn to do right"*
> *(Isaiah 1:15-17).*

millstone instead of a milestone," to quote Vance Havner. At least 62 percent of the people Barna surveyed said that the church was not relevant to today's world and is losing its influence on society. (See *The Frog in the Kettle* by George Barna, published by Regal Books.) It may be that, like the worshipers in the ancient Jewish temple, we are only going through the motions.

Applying God's Truth:

1. In what ways are many Christians today "religious," yet with their hearts "far from God"?

2. Would you say you live in "a Christian nation"? Explain.

3. What do you think is the #1 problem in the church today?

DAY 5

Read **Isaiah 4—6**

Isaiah's Vision

Anyone reading the first few chapters of Isaiah's book might be inclined to ask, "What right does this man have to pronounce judgment on the leaders of our land and the many worshipers in the temple?" The answer is in chapter 6: Isaiah's account of his call to ministry. Before he announced any "woes" on others, he first confessed his own sin and said, "Woe is me!" He saw the Holy One of Israel, and he could not keep silent.

The sight of a holy God, and the sound of the holy hymn of worship, brought great conviction to Isaiah's heart, and he confessed that he was a sinner. Unclean lips are caused by an unclean heart (Matt. 12:34-35). Isaiah cried out to be cleansed inwardly, and God met his need. If this scene had been on earth, the coals would have come from the brazen altar where the sacrificial blood had been shed, or perhaps from the censer of the high priest on the Day of Atonement (Lev. 16:12). Isaiah's cleansing came by blood and fire, and it was verified by the word of the Lord.

Before we can minister to others, we must permit God to minister to us. Before we pronounce "woe"

> *"Then I heard the voice of the Lord saying,*
> *'Whom shall I send? And who will go for Us?'*
> *And I said, 'Here am I. Send me!'"*
> *(Isaiah 6:8)*

upon others, we must sincerely say, "Woe is me!" Isaiah's conviction led to confession, and confession led to cleansing (1 John 1:9).

"Go and tell" is still God's command to His people. He is waiting for us to reply, "Here am I. Send me."

Applying God's Truth:

1. Do you think today's servants of God are "called" as clearly as Isaiah was? If not, how can they be as sure as Isaiah was that they're doing God's will?

2. Do you feel fully equipped and qualified to "go" wherever God sends you? If not, what would need to be done first?

3. Aside from feeling qualified, are you *willing* to say, "Here am I. Send me"? Explain.

DAY 6

Read **Isaiah 7–8**

A Sure Sign

These were perilous days for the nation of Judah. Assyria was growing stronger and threatening the smaller nations whose security depended on a very delicate political balance. Syria and Ephraim (the Northern Kingdom) tried to pressure Judah into an alliance against Assyria, but Ahaz refused to join them. Why? Because he had secretly made a treaty with Assyria! (2 Kings 16:5-9)

If Ahaz had believed God's promise, he would have broken his alliance and called the nation to prayer and praise, but the king continued in his unbelief. Realizing the weakness of the king's faith, Isaiah offered to give a sign to encourage him. But knowing that he was secretly allied with Assyria, how could Ahaz honestly ask the Lord for a special sign? So, instead of speaking only to the king, Isaiah addressed the whole "house of David" and gave the prophecy concerning "Immanuel."

Of course, the *ultimate* fulfillment of this prophecy is in our Lord Jesus Christ, who is "God with us." The virgin birth of Christ is a key doctrine; for if Jesus Christ is not God come in sinless human flesh, then we

> *"The Lord Himself will give you a sign: The virgin will be with child and will give birth to a son, and will call him Immanuel"*
> *(Isaiah 7:14).*

....

have no Savior. However, this "sign" had an *immediate* significance to Ahaz and the people of Judah. A woman who was then a virgin would get married, conceive, and bear a son whose name would be "Immanuel." This son would be a reminder that God was with His people and would care for them. It is likely that this virgin was Isaiah's second wife, his first wife having died after his first son was born, and that Isaiah's second son was named both "Immanuel" and "Maher-shalal-hash-baz."

Applying God's Truth:

1. Do you identify with any of the weaknesses of King Ahaz? In what ways?

2. What changes might you make in your life if you more fully believed God's promise(s)?

3. What are some clear "signs" that God is active in your life?

DAY 7

Read *Isaiah 9–12*

Come Again

The Redeemer will come and bring to the world the dawning of a new day. We know that this prophecy refers to Christ because of the way it is quoted in Matthew 4:13-15. But Isaiah looked beyond the first coming of Christ to His second coming and the establishing of His righteous kingdom.

Isaiah 9:6 declares both the *humanity* ("A Child is born") and the *deity* ("A Son is given") of the Lord Jesus Christ. The prophet then leaps ahead to the Kingdom Age when the Messiah will reign in righteousness and justice from David's throne. God had promised David that his dynasty and throne would be established forever, and this is fulfilled literally in Jesus Christ, who will one day reign from Jerusalem.

If His name is "Wonderful," then there will be nothing dull about His reign! As Counselor, He has the wisdom to rule justly; as the Mighty God, He has the power to execute His wise plans. "Everlasting Father" does not suggest that the Son is also the Father, for each person in the Godhead is distinct. "Father of Eternity" is a better translation. Among the Jews, the word *father* means "originator" or "source."

> *"For to us a child is born, to us a son is given, and the government will be on His shoulders. And He will be called Wonderful Counselor, Mighty God, Everlasting Father, Prince of Peace"*
> *(Isaiah 9:6).*

For example, Satan is the "father [originator] of lies" (John 8:44). If you want anything eternal, you must get it from Jesus Christ; He is the "Father of eternity."

Applying God's Truth:

1. Isaiah saw not only the *coming* of Christ, but His *second coming* as well. How might your spiritual life change if you focused more on the future?

2. What do you most appreciate about the *humanity* of Jesus? What do you appreciate about His *deity*?

3. Of the titles given the Messiah, which gives you most encouragement? Why?

DAY 8

Read *Isaiah 13—18*

The Mighty Keep Falling

Isaiah warned that the kingdom of Judah would be taken into captivity by Babylon, and this happened in 586 B.C. Jeremiah prophesied that the Captivity would last for seventy years. Then Babylon would be judged and the Jews permitted to go home (Jer. 25:1-14). So, the capture of Babylon by Darius would be good news to the Jews, for it would mean the end of their exile and bondage.

The picture in Isaiah 14:1-23 is that of a mighty monarch whose pride brought him to destruction. This is what happened to Belshazzar when Darius the Mede captured Babylon in 539 B.C. Isaiah described the king's arrival in sheol, the world of the dead, where the king's wealth, glory, and power vanished. The dead kings already in sheol stood in tribute to him (14:9), but it was all a mockery. Death is the great leveler; there are no kings in the world of the dead. "Lucifer" (v. 12) is Latin for "morning star" and suggests that this king's glory did not last very long. The morning star shines but is soon swallowed up by the light of the sun.

The name "Lucifer" also indicates that Satan tries

*"How you have fallen from heaven,
O morning star, son of the dawn!
You have been cast down to the earth,
you who once laid low the nations!"*
(Isaiah 14:12)

....

to imitate Jesus Christ, who is the "bright Morning Star" (Rev. 22:16). "I will be like the Most High" reveals his basic strategy, for he is an imitator. Like the king of Babylon, Satan will one day be humiliated and defeated. He will be cast out of heaven and finally cast into hell. Whether God is dealing with kings or angels, Proverbs 16:18 is still true: "Pride goes before destruction, a haughty spirit before a fall."

Applying God's Truth:

1. What was the difference between the "fall" of Judah (God's people) and the "falls" of the surrounding Gentile nations?

2. In what ways do some people today sinfully strive to "be like the Most High"?

3. What's the difference between the desire to "be like the Most High" and a Christian's attempt to be more "Christlike?

DAY 9

Read *Isaiah 19–23*

International News

Chapters 13 through 23 of Isaiah teach us some important lessons. First, *God is in control of the nations of the world, and He can do with them what He pleases.* "Though the mills of God grind slowly, yet they grind exceeding small" (Friedrich von Logau, translated by Henry Wadsworth Longfellow). Second, *God especially hates the sin of pride.* (See Isa. 13:11; 16:6; 23:9; and Prov. 8:13.) When nations turn from the living God to trust their wealth and their armaments, God must show them that He is the only sure refuge. Third, *God judges the nations for the way they treat each other.* Judah was the only nation mentioned that had God's Law, yet God held the other ten Gentile nations accountable for what they did. Finally, *God always gives a word of promise and hope to His people.* Babylon will fall, but God will care for Judah (Isa. 14:1-3, 32). Moab will not accept sanctuary from Jerusalem, but God will one day establish Messiah's throne there (16:5). Assyria and Egypt may be avowed enemies of the Jews, but one day the three nations will together glorify God (19:23-25).

Therefore, no matter how frightening the national or international situation may become, God's children

> *"In that day Israel will be the third,
> along with Egypt and Assyria,
> a blessing on the earth"*
> *(Isaiah 19:24).*

can have peace because they know Almighty God is on His throne. The nations may rage and plot against God, but "The One enthroned in heaven laughs" (Ps. 2:4). When the Lord of heaven and earth is your Father, and you gladly wear Christ's yoke, you have nothing to fear.

Applying God's Truth:

1. When you consider the turmoil around the world, what are some of your biggest fears?

2. What difference does it make in your personal life to believe that "God is in control of the nations of the world"?

3. In spite of national and international problems, what would you say is God's "word of promise and hope" to His people today?

DAY 10

Read *Isaiah 24—25*

Seeking Refuge

Isaiah paints two pictures: the buffeting wind of a storm and the burning rays of the sun in the desert. Where can travelers go for refuge? They see a huge rock and find refuge in it. God is that Rock, and He will be a refuge for His believing people during that terrible "Day of the Lord." The victory shouts of the enemy will disappear the way heat vanishes when a cloud covers the sea.

God cares for His own in times of trial and judgment. He kept Noah and his family alive through the Flood and guarded Israel when His judgments fell on Egypt. He protected believing Rahab and her family when Jericho fell and preserved a faithful remnant when Judah was taken into Babylonian Captivity. Throughout the centuries, He has kept His church in spite of the attacks of Satan and will deliver His church from the wrath to come. When "the Day of the Lord" comes to this godless world, God will see to it that the Jewish remnant will be preserved. "Hide yourselves for a little while until His wrath has passed by. See, the Lord is coming out of His dwelling to punish the people of the earth for their sins" (Isa. 26:20-21).

"You have been a refuge for the poor, a refuge for the needy in his distress, a shelter from the storm and a shade from the heat"
(Isaiah 25:4).

Applying God's Truth:

1. What are some of the current "storms" in your life — the emotionally upsetting situations you face?

2. What are your current sources of "heat" — stress, pressure, and so forth?

3. In what ways is God a refuge for each of the situations you've listed? How can you more fully experience His loving protection?

DAY 11

Read **Isaiah 26—27**

The Grapes of Resistance

Isaiah sees both the Israel of his day and the Israel of the future day when God's kingdom will be established. God was not angry with His people; He just yearned for them to return to Him and fervently trust Him. He used war (Assyria) to punish the Northern Kingdom and Captivity (Babylon) to discipline the Southern Kingdom, but He did this in love and not in anger.

In "the Day of the Lord," God will use suffering to purge His people and prepare them for their kingdom. Isaiah 27:9 does not suggest that personal suffering can atone for sin, for only the sacrifice of Jesus Christ can do that. God uses suffering as a discipline to bring us to submission so that we will seek Him and His holiness (Heb. 12:1-11). The Babylonian Captivity cured the Jews of their idolatry once and for all.

In Isaiah's day, the vineyard was producing wild grapes, but in the future kingdom, Israel will be fruitful and flourishing. God will guard His people and give them all that they need to bring glory to His name. The nation will "bud and blossom and fill all the world with fruit" (v. 6).

> *"Sing about a fruitful vineyard: I, the*
> *LORD, watch over it; I water it continually.*
> *I guard it day and night so that*
> *no one may harm it. I am not angry"*
> *(Isaiah 27:2-4).*

The Bible speaks of three vines: the people of Israel (Isa. 5; 27), Christ and His church (John 15), and godless Gentile society, "the vine of the earth" (Rev. 14:18). The vineyard of Israel is not bearing fruit, the "vine of the earth" is filling the world with poisonous fruit, and God's people must be faithful branches in the Vine and produce fruit that glorifies God's name.

Applying God's Truth:

1. How would you describe your current spiritual life in terms of a vineyard?

2. What are some evidences of "fruit" due to God's involvement in your life?

3. Looking back, can you see how God has worked to make you more productive for Him? Can you cite specific instances?

DAY 12

Read **Isaiah 28**

Misusing a Good Gift

Like all devout Jews, Isaiah loved Jerusalem, the holy city, the city of David, the place of God's dwelling. But Isaiah saw storm clouds gathering over the city and announced that trouble was coming. He began his message announcing God's judgment on Ephraim (28:1-6). Their arrogance was detestable to God, for they thought their fortress city of Samaria was impregnable. Samaria reigned in luxury and pleasure and had no fear of her enemies.

The Lord was also appalled by their drunkenness. To the Jews, wine was a gift from God and a source of joy. The Law did not demand total abstinence, but it did warn against drunkenness.

A government official in Washington, D.C. once quipped, "We have three parties in this city: the Democratic Party, the Republican Party, and the cocktail party." Indeed, Washington D.C. ranks high on the list of cities noted for alcohol consumption. Many people don't realize that alcohol and nicotine, America's favorite legal narcotics, do far more damage than all the illegal drugs combined. According to Dr. Arnold Washton, alcohol and nicotine kill 450,000

> *"Priests and prophets stagger from beer and are befuddled with wine; they reel from beer, they stagger when seeing visions, they stumble when rendering decisions"*
> (Isaiah 28:7).

people annually, while illegal drugs kill about 6,000 (*Willpower's Not Enough,* Harper & Row, 1989, p. 13). What hope is there for our affluent, pleasure-loving society that gives lip service to religion and ignores the tragic consequences of sin and the judgment that is sure to come?

Applying God's Truth:

1. What would you say if a non-Christian friend asked, "What does the Bible say about drinking?"

2. Drunkenness was related to arrogance for the people of Ephraim. Do you think the two traits are still related? In what ways?

3. What advice and/or warning would you give a young person just beginning to start drinking on a regular basis? What would you tell an adult who seems to be addicted?

DAY 13

Read **Isaiah 29**

Awaiting God's Balance

Isaiah asked the people to look ahead and consider what God had planned for them. In their political strategy, they had turned things upside down, but God would one day turn everything around by establishing His glorious kingdom on earth. The devastated land would become a paradise, the disabled would be healed, and the outcasts would be enriched and rejoice in the Lord. There would be no more scoffers or ruthless people practicing injustice in the courts. The founders of the nation, Abraham and Jacob, would see their many descendants all glorifying the Lord.

In light of this glorious future, why should Judah turn to feeble nations like Egypt for help? God is on their side, and they can trust Him! God cared for Jacob during all of his years of trial, and surely He could care for Jacob's children. It is tragic when a nation forgets its great spiritual heritage and turns from trusting the Lord to trusting the plans and promises of men.

At the Constitutional Convention in Philadelphia in 1787, Benjamin Franklin said, "I have lived, sir, a long time, and the longer I live, the more convincing the

DAY 14

Read **Isaiah 30–31**

Whom Do You Trust?

Judah's faith was in men, not in God. They trusted in the legs of horses and the wheels of chariots, not in the hand of the Lord. Why should the Lord fear the Assyrians? Does a lion fear a flock of sheep and their shepherds? Do the eagles fear as they hover over their young in the nest? God will pounce on Assyria like a lion and swoop down like an eagle, and that will be the end! In one night, the Assyrian army was wiped out (Isa. 37:36).

Think of the money Judah would have saved and the distress they would have avoided had they only rested in the Lord their God and obeyed His will. All their political negotiations were futile and their treaties worthless. They could trust the words of the Egyptians but not the Word of God!

As God's church today faces enemies and challenges, it is always a temptation to turn to the world or the flesh for help. But our first response must be to examine our hearts to see if there is something we need to confess and make right. Then we must turn to the Lord in faith and obedience and surrender to His will alone. We must trust Him to protect us and fight for us.

DAY 15

Read **Isaiah 32–33**

A Hopeful Forecast

In 1919, American writer Lincoln Steffens visited the Soviet Union to see what the Communist revolution was accomplishing. In a letter to a friend, he wrote, "I have seen the future, and it works." If he were alive today, he would probably be less optimistic, but in those days, "the Russian experiment" seemed to be dramatically successful.

A university professor posted a sign on his study wall that read, "The future is not what it used to be." Since the advent of atomic energy, many people wonder if there is any future at all. Albert Einstein said that he never thought about the future because it came soon enough!

In Isaiah 32–35, the prophet invites us to look at future events to see what God has planned for His people and His world. In Isaiah 32:1, Isaiah writes about *"a king,"* but in 33:17, he calls him *"the king."* By the time you get to verse 22 in that chapter, He is *"our king."* It is not enough to say that Jesus Christ is "a king" or even *"the* King." We must confess our faith in Him and say with assurance that He is "our King."

> *"Assyria will fall by a sword that is not of man; a sword, not of mortals, will devour them"*
> *(Isaiah 31:8).*

....

A friend of mine kept a card on his office desk that read: Faith Is Living without Scheming. In one statement, that is what Isaiah was saying to Judah and Jerusalem, and that is what he is saying to us today.

Applying God's Truth:

1. Do you agree that "faith is living without scheming"? What, exactly, do you think that means?

2. What can you do to remain patient and faithful while waiting for God to act on your behalf?

3. What are some sources of help that even good people tend to turn to rather than trusting God?

> *"Once more the humble will rejoice in the LORD; the needy will rejoice in the Holy One of Israel. The ruthless will vanish, the mockers will disappear"*
> *(Isaiah 29:19-20).*

proofs I see of this truth — *that God governs in the affairs of men.* I therefore beg leave to move that henceforth prayers imploring the assistance of heaven and its blessings on our deliberations be held in this Assembly every morning. . . ."

Isaiah sought that attitude in Jerusalem, but instead, he found only scoffing and unbelief.

Applying God's Truth:

1. Have you ever gotten yourself in trouble by making a bad alliance with a person or group rather than seeking God's help? What were the circumstances?

2. Are you currently in any cumbersome situations that you would like to be free of? What do you think God would have you do?

3. How can you ensure that your future decisions will reflect God's will for your life rather than someone else's?

> *"The LORD is our judge, the LORD is our lawgiver, the LORD is our king; it is He who will save us"*
> *(Isaiah 33:22).*

In contrast to the evil rulers of Isaiah's day, the Messiah will reign in *righteousness* and *justice*, like a rock of refuge and a refreshing river in the desert.

Isaiah ministered to spiritually blind, deaf, and ignorant people, but in the kingdom, all will see and hear God's truth as well as understand and obey it. This will happen because the nation will have a new heart and enter into a New Covenant with the Lord.

Applying God's Truth:

1. What people do you know who would agree that Jesus is *a* king? *The* King? *Our* King?

2. Right this minute, what are some of your worries about the future? If you *really* trust God, why do you think you're still worried?

3. In what ways has God been like "a refreshing river in the desert" for you in the past? What does that suggest about your future?

DAY 16

Read *Isaiah 34—35*

The Road Less Traveled

Isaiah 35:8 expresses one of Isaiah's favorite themes: the highway (11:16; 19:23; 40:3; 62:10). During the Assyrian invasion, the highways were not safe (33:8), but during the Kingdom Age it will be safe to travel. There will be one special highway: "The Way of Holiness." In ancient cities, there were often special roads that only kings and priests could use, but when Messiah reigns, *all of His people* will be invited to use this highway. Isaiah pictures God's redeemed, ransomed, and rejoicing Jewish families going up to the yearly feasts in Jerusalem, to praise their Lord.

When Isaiah spoke and wrote these words, it is likely that the Assyrians had ravaged the land, destroyed the crops, and made the highways unsafe for travel. The people were cooped up in Jerusalem, wondering what would happen next. The remnant was trusting God's promises and praying for God's help, and God answered their prayers. If God kept His promises to His people centuries ago and delivered them, will He not keep His promises in the future and establish His glorious kingdom for His chosen people? Of course He will!

> *"A highway will be there; it will be called the Way of Holiness. The unclean will not journey on it; it will be for those who walk in that Way"*
>
> *(Isaiah 35:8).*

....

The future is your friend when Jesus Christ is your Savior.

Applying God's Truth:

1. In what way is your spiritual journey like going down a highway?

2. Do you feel completely safe as you travel the "Way of Holiness"? If not, how could you feel safer?

3. How can you be sure you stay on the right highway without taking any wrong turns?

DAY 17

Read **Isaiah 36**

A King to Relate To

Except for David and Solomon, no king of Judah is given more attention in Scripture than Hezekiah. "Hezekiah trusted in the LORD, the God of Israel. There was no one like him among all the kings of Judah, either before him or after him" (2 Kings 18:5).

He began his reign about 715 B.C., though he may have been coregent with his father as early as 729 B.C. He restored the temple facilities and services of worship, destroyed the idols, and sought to bring the people back to vital faith in the Lord. He led the people in a nationwide two-week celebration of Passover and invited Jews from the Northern Kingdom to participate.

After the fall of the Northern Kingdom in 722 B.C., Judah had constant problems with Assyria. Hezekiah finally rebelled against Assyria (2 Kings 18:7), and when Sennacherib threatened to attack, Hezekiah tried to bribe him with tribute (vv. 13-16). It was a lapse of faith on Hezekiah's part that God could not bless. Sennacherib accepted the treasures but broke the treaty (Isa. 33:1) and invaded Judah in 701 B.C. The account of God's miraculous deliverance of His people is given in chapters 36–37.

> *"In the fourteenth year of King Hezekiah's reign, Sennacherib king of Assyria attacked all the fortified cities of Judah and captured them"*
>
> *(Isaiah 36:1).*

....

Chapters 36–39 teach us some valuable lessons about faith, prayer, and the dangers of pride. Though the setting today may be different, the problems and temptations are still the same; for Hezekiah's history is our history, and Hezekiah's God is our God.

Applying God's Truth:

1. Prior to this reading, how much did you know about King Hezekiah? (For further research, see 2 Kings 18–20; 2 Chronicles 29–32; and Isa. 36–39.)

2. When you, like Hezekiah, "inherit" something that all your predecessors have made a mess of, do you tend to do what's easy and go with the flow, or do what's hard and correct the situation?

3. What do you think made Hezekiah so different from the kings who preceded him? What can you learn from his example?

DAY 18

Read **Isaiah 37**

No Problem Too Big

Sennacherib boasted of his military might and his great conquests, for no obstacle stood in his way. If he so desired, like a god, he could even dry up the rivers! But the king of Assyria forgot that he was only God's tool for accomplishing His purposes on the earth, and the tool must not boast against the Maker (Isa. 10:5-19). God would humble Sennacherib and his army by treating them like cattle and leading them away from Jerusalem (Isa. 37:7, 29).

The Assyrian field commander had joked that one Assyrian junior officer was stronger than 2,000 Jewish charioteers (Isa. 36:8-9), but it took *only one* of God's angels to destroy 185,000 Assyrian soldiers! Isaiah had prophesied the destruction of the Assyrian army. God would mow them down like a forest (10:33-34), devastate them with a storm (Isa. 30:27-30), and throw them into the fire like garbage on the city dump (vv. 31-33).

But that was not all. After Sennacherib left Judah, a defeated man, he returned to his capital city of Nineveh. Twenty years later, as a result of a power struggle among his sons, Sennacherib was

> *"The angel of the Lord went out and put to death a hundred and eighty-five thousand men in the Assyrian camp. . . . So Sennacherib king of Assyria broke camp and withdrew"*
> *(Isaiah 37:36-37).*

assassinated by two of his sons in fulfillment of Isaiah's prophecy (Isa. 37:7), and it happened in the temple of his god! The field commander had ridiculed the gods of the nations, but Sennacherib's own god could not protect him.

Applying God's Truth:

1. Do you know bullies like Sennacherib? How do you handle such abusive people?

2. How do you feel when you seem tremendously outnumbered? Why?

3. What can you learn from this story to apply to stressful situations you're currently facing?

DAY 19

Read *Isaiah 38—39*

Miracle Recovery

Hezekiah was an author of psalms (Isa. 38:20) and supervised a group of scholars who copied the Old Testament Scriptures (Prov. 25:1). In the beautiful meditation in Isaiah 38, the king tells us how he felt during his experience of illness and recovery. He had some new experiences that made him a better person.

For one thing, God gave him *a new appreciation of life* (vv. 9-12). We take life for granted till it is about to be taken from us, and then we cling to it as long as we can. Hezekiah pictured death as the end of a journey, a tent taken down, and a weaving cut from the loom. Life was hanging by a thread!

He also had *a new appreciation of prayer* (vv. 13-14). Were it not for prayer, Hezekiah could not have made it. At night, the king felt like a frail animal being attacked by a fierce lion; in the daytime, he felt like a helpless bird. During this time of suffering, Hezekiah examined his own heart and confessed his sins, and God forgave him.

The king ended with *a new appreciation of opportunities for service* (vv. 15-20). There was a new

> *"In those days Hezekiah became ill and was at the point of death. The prophet Isaiah son of Amoz went to him and said, 'This is what the L*ORD *says: Put your house in order, because you are going to die; you will not recover'"*
>
> *(Isaiah 38:1).*

....

humility in his walk, a deeper love for the Lord in his heart, and a new song of praise on his lips. He had a new determination to praise God all the days of his life, for now those days were very important to him.

Applying God's Truth:

1. Since Isaiah was God's prophet, and God's prophets were always correct, why do you think Hezekiah prayed for more time after God said he would not recover?

2. Do you think this is a case where God actually changed His mind? Explain.

3. What can you remember from this story the next time you're facing a seemingly hopeless and final situation?

DAY 20

Read **Isaiah 40:1-26**

Reading the IBV (Isaiah Bible Version)

The Book of Isaiah can be called "a Bible in miniature." There are sixty-six chapters in Isaiah and sixty-six books in the Bible. The thirty-nine chapters in the first part of Isaiah may be compared to the Old Testament with its thirty-nine books, and both focus primarily on God's judgment of sin. The twenty-seven chapters of the second part may be seen to parallel the twenty-seven books of the New Testament, and both emphasize the grace of God.

The "New Testament" section of Isaiah opens with the ministry of John the Baptist (40:3-5; Mark 1:1-4) and closes with the new heavens and the new earth (Isa. 65:17; 66:22). At the heart of the "New Testament" section of Isaiah's book is our Lord Jesus Christ and His sacrifice on the cross for our sins. No wonder Isaiah has been called "the evangelical prophet."

As you study Isaiah 40–66, keep in mind that it was originally addressed to a group of discouraged Jewish refugees who faced a long journey home and a difficult task when they got there. Note how often God says to them, "Fear not!" and how frequently He assures them

> *"Comfort, comfort My people, says your God. . . . The grass withers and the flowers fall, but the word of our God stands forever"*
> *(Isaiah 40:1, 8).*

....

of His pardon and His presence. It is no surprise that God's people for centuries have turned to these chapters to find assurance and encouragement in the difficult days of life; for in these messages, God says to all of His people, "Be comforted!"

Applying God's Truth:

1. Isaiah's message was that something better was coming in the future. Do God's people still need that message? Why?

2. In what ways do you relate with people who are discouraged and have difficult tasks?

3. How many circumstances can you think of where you long to hear God say, "Fear not! Be comforted!"?

DAY 21

Read **Isaiah 40:27—44:28**

Plod While You Wait

God knows how we feel and what we fear, and He is adequate to meet our every need. We can never obey God in our own strength, but we can always trust Him to provide the strength we need (Phil 4:13). If we trust ourselves, we will faint and fall, but if we wait on the Lord by faith, we will receive strength for the journey. The word *wait* (KJV) does not suggest that we do nothing. It means "to hope," to look to God for all that we need. This involves meditating on His character and His promises, praying, and seeking to glorify Him.

The word *renew* means "to exchange," as taking off old clothes and putting on new. We exchange our weakness for His power (2 Cor. 12:1-10). As we wait before Him, God enables us to soar when there is a crisis, to run when the challenges are many, and to walk faithfully in the day-by-day demands of life. *It is much harder to walk in the ordinary pressures of life than to fly like the eagle in a time of crisis.*

"I can plod," said William Carey, the father of modern missions. "That is my only genius. I can persevere in any definite pursuit. To this I owe everything."

"Those who hope in the LORD will renew their strength. They will soar on wings like eagles; they will run and not grow weary, they will walk and not be faint"
(Isaiah 40:31).

....

The greatest heroes of faith are not always those who seem to be soaring; often they are the ones who are patiently plodding. As we wait on the Lord, He enables us not only to fly higher and run faster, but also to *walk longer.* Blessed are the plodders, for they eventually arrive at their destination!

Applying God's Truth:

1. What do you find most difficult about waiting upon and hoping in the Lord? Why?

2. When are some times you have flown like an eagle during a crisis?

3. What are three things you can do to be sure you keep plodding ahead *every* day?

DAY 22

Read **Isaiah 45—48**

Get Out of Babylon!

The Jews had become comfortable and complacent in their Captivity and did not want to leave. They had followed the counsel of Jeremiah (Jer. 29:4-7) and had houses, gardens, and families; it would not be easy for them to pack up and go to the holy land. *But that was where they belonged and where God had a work for them to do.* God told them that they were hypocritical in using His name and identifying with His city but not obeying His will (Isa. 48:1-2). They were stubborn and were not excited about the new things God was doing for them.

Had they obeyed the Lord in the first place, they would have experienced peace and not war (vv. 18-19), but it was not too late. He had put them into the furnace to refine them and prepare them for their future work. "Leave Babylon" was God's command (v. 20). God would go before them and prepare the way, and they had nothing to fear.

One would think that the Jews would be eager to leave their "prison" and return to their land to see God do new and great things for them. They had grown accustomed to the security of bondage and had

> *"See, I have refined you, though not as silver; I have tested you in the furnace of affliction"*
> *(Isaiah 48:10).*

....

forgotten the challenges of freedom. The church today can easily grow complacent with its comfort and affluence. God may have to put us into the furnace to remind us that we are here to be *servants* and not *consumers* or *spectators*.

Applying God's Truth:

1. How do Christians today become complacent with the "captivity" of sin?

2. When were some times you could have avoided a lot of trouble if you had obeyed God "in the first place"?

3. How is your character refined in the "furnace of affliction"?

DAY 23

Read *Isaiah 49*

Gentile Light

Messiah came as both a Servant and a Warrior, serving those who trust Him and ultimately judging those who resist Him. All of God's servants should be like prepared weapons. "It is not great talents God blesses so much as great likeness to Jesus," wrote Robert Murray McCheyne. "A holy minister [servant] is an awful weapon in the hand of God."

The Jewish nation was called to glorify God and be a light to the Gentiles, but they failed in their mission. This is why Messiah is called "Israel" in Isaiah 49:3: He did the work that Israel was supposed to do. Today, the church is God's light in this dark world, and like Israel, we seem to be failing in our mission to take the Good News to the ends of the earth. We cannot do the job very effectively when only 5 percent of the average local church budget is devoted to evangelism!

As Jesus Christ ministered on earth, especially to Israel, there were times when His work seemed in vain (Isa. 49:4). The religious leaders opposed Him, the disciples did not always understand Him, and those He helped did not always thank Him. He lived and labored by faith, and God gave Him success.

> *"I will also make you a light for the Gentiles, that you may bring My salvation to the ends of the earth"*
> *(Isaiah 49:6).*

....

Our Lord could not minister to the Gentiles until first He ministered to the Jews (vv. 5-6). He was despised by both Jews and Gentiles, but He did God's work and was glorified.

Applying God's Truth:

1. Can you think of any groups of people whom you tend to overlook as potential recipients of the Gospel?

2. In what ways might the "light" of the church shine brighter in today's world?

3. How could your own light brighten a little more gloom than usual today?

DAY 24

Read *Isaiah 50–51*

Complete Submission

The emphasis in this portion of Isaiah is on the Servant's submission to the Lord God in every area of His life and service. His *mind* was submitted to the Lord God so that He could learn His Word and His will (50:4). Everything Jesus said and did was taught to Him by His Father. He prayed to the Father for guidance and meditated on the Word. What God taught the Servant, the Servant shared with those who needed encouragement and help. The Servant sets a good example here for all who know the importance of a daily "quiet time" with the Lord.

The servant's *will* was also yielded to the Lord God. A "wakened ear" (50:4) is one that hears and obeys the voice of the master. The people to whom Isaiah ministered were neither "willing" nor "obedient" (1:19), but the Servant did gladly the will of the Lord God. This was not easy, for it meant yielding His *body* to wicked men who mocked Him, whipped Him, spat on Him, and then nailed Him to a cross.

The Servant did all of this *by faith* in the Lord God. He was determined to do God's will even if it meant going to a cross, for He knew that the Lord God would

> *"Because the Sovereign LORD helps me, I will not be disgraced. Therefore have I set my face like flint, and I know I will not be put to shame"*
> *(Isaiah 50:7).*

help Him. The Servant was falsely accused, but He knew that God would vindicate Him and eventually put His enemies to shame. Keep in mind that when Jesus Christ was ministering here on earth, He had to live by faith even as we must today. He did not use His divine powers selfishly for Himself but trusted God and depended on the power of the Spirit.

Applying God's Truth:

1. Do you need to more fully submit your mind to God? Your will? Your body? How can you make any needed changes?

2. What connections do you detect between faith and submission?

3. How does feeling disgrace or shame affect your spiritual growth? How can you deal with any problems in these areas?

DAY 25

Read *Isaiah 52*

Sounds of Silence

The people whose mouths dropped open with astonishment at the Servant's humiliation and exaltation will shut their mouths in guilt when they hear His proclamation. Paul interprets this as the preaching of the Gospel to the Gentile nations (Rom. 15:20-21). "So that every mouth may be silenced and the whole world held accountable to God" (Rom. 3:19).

Many people have been tortured and killed, but knowing about their suffering does not touch our conscience, though it might arouse our sympathy. Our Lord's sufferings and death were different because *they involved everybody in the world.* The Gospel message is not "Christ died," for that is only a fact in history, like "Napoleon died." The Gospel message is that "Christ died *for our sins*" (1 Cor. 15:1-4, italics mine). You and I are as guilty of Christ's death as Annas and Caiaphas, Herod Antipas, and Pilate.

Now we see why people are astonished when they understand the message of the Gospel. This Man whom they condemned has declared that *they are condemned* unless they turn from sin and trust Him.

> *"So will He sprinkle many nations, and kings will shut their mouths because of Him"*
> *(Isaiah 52:15).*

....

You cannot rejoice in the Good News of salvation until you face the bad news of condemnation. Jesus did not suffer and die because He was guilty, but because *we* were guilty. People are astonished at this fact; it shuts their mouths.

Applying God's Truth:

1. Can you recall a time when you received news that left you completely speechless?

2. What are some problems that you know about, yet haven't really touched your conscience?

3. How do you feel when you dwell on the fact that Christ died for *your* sins?

DAY 26

Read **Isaiah 53**

Sinless and Silent

Isaiah 53:7 speaks of Jesus' silence under suffering and verse 8 of His silence when illegally tried and condemned to death. In today's courts, a person can be found guilty of terrible crimes, but if it can be proved that something in the trial was illegal, the case must be tried again. *Everything* about Jesus' trials was illegal, but He did not appeal for another trial.

The Servant is compared to a lamb, which is one of the frequent symbols of the Savior in Scripture. A lamb died for each Jewish household at Passover, and the Servant died for His people, the nation of Israel. Jesus is "the Lamb of God, who takes away the sin of the world" (John 1:29); twenty-eight times in the Book of Revelation, Jesus is referred to as the Lamb.

Since Jesus Christ was crucified *with* criminals *as* a criminal, it was logical that His dead body would be left unburied, but God had other plans. The burial of Jesus Christ is as much a part of the Gospel as is His death, for the burial is proof that He actually died. The Roman authorities would not have released the body to Joseph and Nicodemus if the victim were not dead. A wealthy man like Joseph would never carve out a

> *"He was oppressed and afflicted, yet He did not open His mouth; He was led like a lamb to the slaughter, and as a sheep before her shearers is silent, so He did not open His mouth"*
> *(Isaiah 53:7).*

tomb for himself so near to a place of execution, particularly when his home was miles away. He prepared it for Jesus and had the spices and graveclothes ready for the burial. How wonderfully God fulfilled Isaiah's prophecy!

Applying God's Truth:

1. Many times Jesus' words had silenced His opponents. Why do you think He remained silent at His trial?

2. In what ways is a lamb a good symbol for Jesus? In each case, can you make the same application to *yourself*?

3. How do you feel when you are condemned for something you didn't do? What can you learn from Jesus' response in the same situation?

DAY 27

Read *Isaiah 54—56*

The #1 Thirst Quencher

The invitation to come to the waters is extended to "everyone" and not just to the Jews. Anyone who is thirsting for that which really satisfies is welcome to come. As in Isaiah 25:6, the prophet pictures God's blessings in terms of a great feast, where God is the host.

In the East, water is a precious ingredient, and an abundance of water is a special blessing. Wine, milk, and bread were staples of their diet. The people were living on substitutes that did not nourish them. They needed "the real thing" which only the Lord could give. In Scripture, both water and wine are pictures of the Holy Spirit (John 7:37-39; Eph. 5:18). Jesus is the "bread of life" (John 6:32-35), and His living Word is like milk (1 Peter 2:2). Our Lord probably had Isaiah 55:2 in mind when He said, "Do not work for food that spoils, but for food that endures to eternal life" (John 6:27).

People have to work hard to dig wells, care for flocks and herds, plant seed, and tend to the vineyards. But the Lord offers to them *free* everything they are laboring for. If they listen to His Word, they

> *"Come, all you who are thirsty, come to the waters. . . . Come, buy wine and milk without money and without cost"*
>
> *(Isaiah 55:1).*

will be inclined to come; for God draws sinners to Himself through the Word (John 5:24). Note the emphasis on *hearing* in Isaiah 55:2-3. Jesus Christ is God's covenant to the Gentiles ("peoples"), and His promises will stand as long as His Son lives, which is forever.

Applying God's Truth:

1. What is something you have recently been "thirsting" for?

2. How does intense thirst affect your mood and productivity? How might this be true in a spiritual sense as well?

3. What are the "waters" that will eliminate your spiritual thirst? Explain.

DAY 28

Read *Isaiah 57–59*

Truth versus Lies

There was a great deal of injustice in the land, with the rich exploiting the poor and the rulers using their authority only to make themselves rich. The people lifted their hands to worship God, but their hands were stained with blood (1:15, 21). God could not answer their prayers because their sins hid His face from them.

It was a conflict between *truth* and *lies*, just as it is today. When people live on lies, they live in a twilight zone and do not know where they are going. When truth falls, it creates a "traffic jam"; justice and honesty cannot make progress. God is displeased with injustice, and He wonders that none of His people will intercede or intervene (Prov. 24:11-22). So the Lord Himself intervened and brought the Babylonians to destroy Judah and Jerusalem and to teach His people that they cannot despise His Law and get away with it.

God's judgment on His people was a foreshadowing of that final Day of the Lord when all the nations will be judged. When it is ended, Israel will be not only God's *chosen* people but God's *cleansed* people, and the glory of the Lord will radiate from Mt. Zion.

> *"Justice is far from us, and righteousness does not reach us. We look for light, but all is darkness; for brightness, but we walk in deep shadows"*
> *(Isaiah 59:9).*

....

The glory of the Lord in the promised kingdom is the theme of the closing chapters of Isaiah. While we are waiting and praying, "Thy kingdom come," perhaps we should also be interceding and intervening. We are the salt of the earth and the light of the world, and God expects us to make a difference.

Applying God's Truth:

1. What would you say are the primary injustices in today's society?

2. What lies still influence God's people? How do *you* avoid being taken in by them?

3. In what ways are you "interceding and intervening" as you await God's kingdom?

DAY 29

Read **Isaiah 60–62**

Jubilee!

The background of Isaiah 61 is the "Year of Jubilee" described in Leviticus 25:7ff. Every seven years, the Jews were to observe a "sabbatical year" and allow the land to rest. After seven sabbaticals, or forty-nine years, they were to celebrate the fiftieth year as the "Year of Jubilee." During that year, all debts were canceled, all land was returned to the original owners, the slaves were freed, and everybody was given a fresh new beginning. This was the Lord's way of balancing the economy and keeping the rich from exploiting the poor.

If you have trusted Christ as your Savior, you are living today in a spiritual "Year of Jubilee." You have been set free from bondage; your spiritual debt to the Lord has been paid; you are living in "the acceptable year of the Lord." Instead of the ashes of mourning, you have a crown on your head; for He has made you a king (Rev. 1:6). You have been anointed with the oil of the Holy Spirit, and you wear a garment of righteousness.

In her days of rebellion, Israel was like a fading oak and a waterless garden (Isa. 1:30), but in the kingdom, she will be like a watered garden (Isa. 58:11) and a tree

> *"I, the LORD, love justice; I hate robbery and iniquity. In My faithfulness I will reward them and make an everlasting covenant with them"*
> *(Isaiah 61:8).*

(oak) of righteousness (Isa. 61:3). In their kingdom "Year of Jubilee," the Jewish people will rebuild, repair, and restore their land, and the Gentiles will shepherd Israel's flocks and herds and tend to their crops. Instead of being farmers and shepherds, the Jews will be priests and ministers! God will acknowledge them as His firstborn (Ex. 4:22) and give them a double portion of His blessing.

Applying God's Truth:

1. Do you have any kind of system that ensures rest, canceled debts, and settled accounts for others on a regular basis? If not, what are some potential consequences?

2. In what ways do you demonstrate "Jubilee blessings" in your life now?

3. To whom could you provide an unexpected gift of freedom and/or peace?

DAY 30

Read *Isaiah 63–66*

Comfort King

Throughout his book, Isaiah has presented us with alternatives: trust the Lord and live, or rebel against the Lord and die. He has explained the grace and mercy of God and offered His forgiveness. He has also explained the holiness and wrath of God and warned of His judgment. He has promised glory for those who will believe and judgment for those who scoff. He has explained the foolishness of trusting man's wisdom and the world's resources.

The prophet calls the professing people of God back to spiritual reality. He warns against hypocrisy and empty worship. He pleads for faith, obedience, a heart that delights in God, and a life that glorifies God. "There is no peace," says my God, "for the wicked" (Isa. 57:21); for in order to have peace, you must have righteousness. The only way to have righteousness is through faith in Jesus Christ (Rom. 3:19-31).

Isaiah's message has been, "Be comforted by the Lord!" *But God cannot comfort rebels!* If we are sinning against God and comfortable about it, something is radically wrong. That false comfort will lead to false confidence, and that will lead to the

> *"This is the one I esteem: he who is humble and contrite in spirit, and trembles at My word"*
> *(Isaiah 66:2).*

....

chastening hand of God. "Seek the LORD while He may be found" (Isa. 55:6).

"I will praise you, O LORD. Although You were angry with me, Your anger has turned away and You have comforted me" (12:1).

BE COMFORTED!

Applying God's Truth:

1. What are some clear alternatives you're currently facing in your life?

2. In what ways do you still tend to be a rebel in God's kingdom?

3. What three things has Isaiah taught you (or reminded you of) that you feel will be most significant in your near future?